Ethereal Mantras, Affirmations and Notions for Placid and Peaceful Earth Plane Traversal

Ethereal Mantras, Affirmations and Notions for Placid and Peaceful Earth Plane Traversal

Volumes I and II

No One

authorHOUSE®

AuthorHouse™
1663 Liberty Drive
Bloomington, IN 47403
www.authorhouse.com
Phone: 1-800-839-8640

Published by AuthorHouse   05/01/2012

ISBN: 978-1-4685-3951-6 (sc)
ISBN: 978-1-4685-3950-9 (e)

Library of Congress Control Number: 2012900137

Contents/Menu

VOLUME 1

Preamble
Lose the Wait

We humans often delay our ascension by weighting/waiting.

We wait when we use food and other addictions as nourishment,
ego grasp (struggling to obtain), and possess/maintain an "ideal"
(e.g., mate, images, are prideful).
We get caught up in
and distracted by illusions and noises and continue to participate
in sense-pleasure dramas.

When one releases these weights/waits,
thereby becoming "lightened,"
he/she can then

Ascend.

No One

That's right; be no "one."
Evolve/open up to "everyone."
Life is limitless as everyone.

As everyone, you can shamelessly, freely, and easily

Eat:
Sushi, collard greens, cornbread, baklava, quiche, raw oysters,
shepherd's pie, bagels, hummus.
Tofu, steak, brown rice, tamales, and so on . . .

Wear:
Jeans, dashikis, robes, shorts, skirts, suits, dresses,
scarves, earrings, kimonos, sandals, boots, bikinis, gowns, ties,
nothing, and so on . . .

Listen to:
Hip-hop, Bach, jazz, reggae, John Denver, Anita Baker, the blues,
the fat lady, new age, oldies, and so on . . .

Dance:
Waltz, two step, lambda, funky chicken, cabbage patch, the twist,
salsa, and so on . . .

Be:
Vulnerable, strong, smart, shy, meek, docile, innocent.
sexy, handsome, emotional, determined, fickle, outspoken,
humble, serious, athletic, tenacious, funny, adaptable,
whimsical, flexible, and so on . . .

Ah, what freedom, spaciousness,
and endless possibilities
As everyone.

Illusion and Noise

Everything and everyone outside of you is
illusion and noise.

Sometimes the illusions are unsightly, unattractive, and ugly,
But they are also at times alluring, attractive, and haunting.

Sometimes the noises are harmonious, beautiful, and soothing,
Whereas at other times they are discordant, upsetting, and
displeasing.

Peace, Bliss, and Happiness

Inner peace
makes possible inner bliss,
which creates ultimate happiness.

Ownership

You do not belong to your
Gender,
Race,
Culture,
Religion,
City,
State,
County,
Country,
Parents,
Partner,
Lover,
Children,
Government,
Sexuality,
Political party/affiliation,
Social class,
School,
College,
Occupation,
Significant other,
Spouse,
Or any others you can think of.

You belong only to self, hence, primary loyalty

Is to_____;

Therefore, it is permissible and okay to say
no to any or all of them.

True fulfillment and happiness will be yours, see,
When you are able to say no to others and yes to thee.

Bliss Is Effortless

Examining, selecting, squeezing, washing, cutting, mixing,
chopping,
stirring, folding, blending, boiling, grating, sampling, tasting,
baking, braising, seasoning, pouring, and serving.

End drinking and eating.
"Bliss is effortless."

Lying, phoning, driving, buying, sneaking, smelling, rolling,
lighting, smoking, measuring, spooning, heating, scraping, lining,
snorting, huffing, puffing, tensing, loading,
injecting,
pouring, mixing, drinking, popping.

End high or low.
"Bliss is effortless."

Working, posing, flexing, pumping, performing,
acting,
dancing, writing, composing, drawing, practicing, painting,
stitching, sewing, running, jumping, playing, swimming,
polishing, shining, singing, displaying.

End ego gratification, praise,
Ribbon, certificate, award, trophy.
"Bliss is effortless"

Preening, posing, flirting, attracting, wooing, posturing,
seducing, wining, dining, cooing, kissing, pawing, rubbing,
grinding, sweating, undulating, grunting, tasting,
mouthing, licking, screaming, yelling,

End orgasm.
"Bliss is effortless."

Dealing

When and if you feel hurt, pain, or anger,
Go inside yourself to heal
instead of outside to deal.

That is, dealing by negative relating and interactions with others
and/or using and abusing food, chemical substances, or your
mental, emotional, or physical body or spirit/soul.

Want

Want is a four-letter word.

Webs and Weapons

Some people use their bodies as webs to snare and trap those craving and hungering for visual and tactile sense pleasure.

And some people use their bodies as weapons to defend against the dis-ease, discord, lack of true self-love, and emptiness within their souls.

Nourishment

Food is not nourishment,
only subsistence for the physical body.

Blissfulness and love (their millions of expressions)
possess the power to nourish all of our bodies,
Emotional, mental, and spiritual.

Wealth

Money is dormant, colored, fibrous paper matter that only
gains its intended worth when it is exchanged and used to express
holistic environmental and humanistic ideals, opinions, and feelings.

These expressions are true wealth because they can create
Connectedness, happiness, and joy.

Rites

Rites of passage are not needed,
Every child/person on the planet has the "right" to be treated
with dignity, respected and valued.

One should not have to reach a certain age or stage of maturation
or prove anything to anybody via accomplishments
or feats to earn the
"Right."

Blast In

People "blast off" to exotic places, retreats, vacations,
relationships, chemical-induced trips, sense pleasures, and myriad
other props as well as the excitement of the dramas,

Only to experience the exhaustion, letdowns, disappointments,
resentments, soreness, crashes, and hangovers when they return
and the play is over.

Blast in
To tap the ever-present and ever-flowing

Contentment and bliss that awaits
just before your true essence.

Higher Love

Lower love is for the love of
Your:
Looks
Social status
Money
Material possessions
Love-making
Ability to fulfill my needs.

Higher love has no rules, contingencies, requirements, conditions, or strings attached.

It is based on another's essence and inner being.

The aforementioned are bonuses.

Judgment

The sharp sword that's disguised often and wielded as a feather duster.

This purported duster cleans tainted, blemished, and tarnished persons, thereby making them "clean."

In actuality, this sword dismembers and cuts one's psychic body, emotional body, self-worth, and self-esteem apart limb by limb.

We also employ it on ourselves whenever we don't accept and honor every aspect of our being (perceived positive and negative) and strive to live up to someone else's expectations, desires, and standards.

Sheathe the sword, embrace and accept yourself, and in turn embrace and accept
All of our fellow inhabitants.

S's

Soliloquy
Silence
Sympathy
Sustenance
Soothing
Sunshine
Sensual
Sound
Sincerity
Social
Sachet
Safe
Sunflower
Sage
Savor
Sail
Salience
Satisfied
Sanctuary
Sated
Serene
Scenic
Scent
Secure
Seed
Self-reliant
Sensate
Sequestered
Service

Silk
Simple
Sky
Simplicity
Skylark
Sleek
Smiles
Snuggle
Soft
Sun
Song
Snore
Splendid
Soul
Spirit
Star
Sprite
Steady
Stern
Still
Stream
Sensitive
Sensational
Synergy
Sweet
Swallow
Supreme
Support
Supple

Super
Succor
Success
Sublime
Suave
Strength
Sonnet
Stellar
Stable
Spring
Solvent
Sexuality
Symphony.

Ego vs. Self-Esteem

Rivals who vie, contend, fight, and compete for prominence in and control of your life.

Shark ego ravages and slaughters others as it gorges itself, never sated, constantly, eagerly searching for ways to feed, devouring any impressionable or weak soul/being in its path.

Dolphin self-esteem navigates placidly and methodically, earning and taking only what it needs for sustenance. Willing and able to help others and is not challenged or threatened by their accolades/successes/prosperity. Dolphin exudes confidence, sensitivity, courtesy, strength, and humbleness.

Who's winning the battle in your life? Fire shark and let dolphin propel and take you to your highest heights.

Love Shade/Shine

Whenever you are fearful or sad because you think
no one cares for or loves you, remember
Mother Earth.
She feeds, shelters, and houses you as long as
you reside in a physical body, soothes you with her waters and
supports you as you walk across her face.

Recall sun, also, the supreme ultimate symbol
and expression of everlasting unconditional love.
It shines love on you when others and even you think
you aren't deserving. It may be obscured by clouds or radiating onto
another portion of the planet, however, like someone out there
in your life, it is ever present and committed to

---

growth and well-being.

Their love also at times may be unseen or unfelt
due to discord, misunderstandings, and confusion,
but, as the sun, it is always there.

Therefore, do not be down, discouraged, or disheartened.
Know that you are loved every second of every moment in every
hour of every day of your existence.

Worthiness

You are worthy, wonderful, special, unique, and valuable
just as you are all of the time no matter what you do or don't do.
This is a given indisputable birthright. Why continue
to listen to those who say

---

is not worthy because of her or his
Social and economic status,
Gender,
Attractiveness,
Sexuality,
Skin color,
Ethnicity,

Height,
Physical challenges,
Political affiliation,
Lack of Ability to do "anything,"
IQ,
Family history or problems,
Percentage of body fat,
Abode, or
Vehicle?

Stop falling for these fallacies, claim and recline in your throne,
wear the crown, *You are Royalty and Worthy*.

Credo/Creed

Attention, pained, angered, bitter, spiteful, hateful, and judgmental beings,
I/we refuse to accept your
Pain,
Anger,
Bitterness,
Spite,
Hate,
And judgments.

Instead I/we shall deflect them and wish for you evolution, peace,
and love.
I/we know that you are only blinded, unaware, and oblivious to
your true essence, which is
Light, love, and goodness.

Perfection

Perfection is the popular, projected illusion that is really poison.

Poison that destroys our sense of self-worth, self-esteem, and confidence by allowing us to think that we are less than, are not good enough, don't measure up, have failed, and are consequently failures.

Purge the poison; know that nothing is truly perfect; hence, you don't have to be either.

Expend effort and energy toward and for your goals, remembering that a steady stream of water cuts fissures and caverns into mountains.

Mastery

To be unmoved by
pretties, problems, praises,
and the host of millions of interactive illusions
that are presented to and for you every second.

Rules and Rituals

The more rules,
The more restrictions.

The more restrictions,
The more restraint.

The more restraint,
The harder respiration,
harder respiration caused by regulated breath.

Rules regulate respiration.

Constricted breath, created by constricted choices or freedoms,
which are chains that bind you/us,

keeps us in line, in synch, and in step with
"right" action(s),
Rituals, holidays, conventions. meccas, ceremonies, festivals,
convergences, and gatherings are times and places for practicing
rules, regardless of sincerity, reasonableness, or sensibility.

Remove your masks; realize that the only rule to live by is to be
loving to self
and in turn others.

Abiding

Be as the rose.

Its roots are your cosmic connections to
spiritual sustenance.

Its stalk is your legs and trunk
Lifting your toward the sun (love).

Its thorns represent your inner fortitude
(created by harmony/peace),
Which shields you and protects you from assailants.

Its petals are your heart, head, and face,
Let them be soft, supple, and open to and for appreciation
of passersby.

Its aroma is your love (courtesy of earth and sun),
channeled by words and actions.
Exude and radiate it indiscriminately
to all earthbound travelers,
As the rose.

VOLUME II

Wholly Holy Holidays

Holi-days or holi-daze? You decide. I say folly craze.

What is holy
about saturating your body with booze
and not working the next day so you can sleep it off?

What is holy
about espousing, mouthing rhetoric about brotherhood/sisterhood,
equality, justice, and unity,
and then continuing your separatist, elitist, racist attitudes and
practices the very next day?
What is holy
about getting all dressed up in your Sunday best (new clothes),
attending church that one special Sunday
and then forgetting about your faith the remainder of the year?
About lying to children, feeding them gobs of sticky, sugary,
chemically flavored jelly beans and chocolate bunnies?

What is holy
about celebrating your country's independence
when the price for it was the annihilation of a race/culture
whose surviving peoples are quarantined on barren, unwanted parcels
of land?,
new taxation probably exceeding the rate forefathers fled their
country for? About exploding chemicals and smoke across bodies of water
and fields?
What is holy
about nations teaching people that it is okay to murder one another
over differing social, religious, political and economic values,
about honoring minorities who gave their lives for the power elite's
goals (earning respect, acceptance) whilst
the survivors still contend with racism and its resultant policies and
practices every day?

What is holy
about kids dressing up
in monster suits, scaring each other? About kids demanding candy
from strangers and defacing or trashing their property if none is given?
About buying a pumpkin, dumping the seeds carving a face in it,
displaying it for two weeks and then tossing it in the garbage
when homeless people are starving on the street?

What is holy
about the Man allowing you a paid day off to be with your family
(sometimes loved ones),
about being nice to family members you can't stand,
doing the good deed of donating food or working in the soup
kitchen so they can have that special meal (homeless) on November
25th and not giving a damn whether they eat the other 364 days of
the year?

What is holy
about importing trinkets, marking them up 300 percent
and then raking
in the bucks as those with the spirit buy, buy, buy? About going into
debt, giving to get, comparing gifts, jealousy,
purchasing war toys and electronic death games for children,
buying and trimming, a tree (that took five to
seven years to grow),
displaying it in your window a month and then tossing it in the trash?
About putting bright lights in your windows, on your door,
the edges of your house and even your lapel/blouse when your
heart is cold
and dark with bigotry (all forms) and contempt toward your fellow
man/woman? About, thousands of people feeling depressed, lonely,
and unloved
because they didn't get a card, a call, an invitation or gift,
some so much so that they do themselves "in"?

Why wait for "their" designated time to express love to some one
you care about,
celebrate and practice your beliefs and demonstrate your values?
Consider celebrating and practicing every day,
make every day of your existence a "holy" day
rather than participating in the folly days crazes.

S.I.C.ness

(socialization indoctrination civilization.)
Past and present American S.I.C.ness facilitates, teaches, breeds, and promotes:

Lemmings—
Greed,
Egoism,
Egocentrism,
Racism,
Sexism,
Homophobia,
Separation,
Competition,
Dis-esteem,
Materialism,
Deceit,
Exploitation,
Hypocrisy,
Aggression,
Violence, and
Hatred.

P.S. My wish for you is that my writings will provide a remedy or cure for the disease.

Walls =/ Hindrances

Neighborhoods, territories, towns, borders, counties, states,
countries, nations, fences, hemispheres.
They only serve the purpose of separation, segregation, the creation
of internal walls, and the elimination
and prevention of the awareness of the one inhalation and
exhalation of the one breath and our one
Blood coursing through our one vein in our one body pumped by
our one heart, which beats in time with our home's (earth's) sounds,
waves, and winds.
Would it were we all tear down these walls, those within and
without and become the one race and one family, expressing the
one love residing on the one earth illuminated by the one sun.

C&C

Listen to the lies; you've heard them, and you've told them:
I didn't get a chance to! I forgot!
I didn't have the time to! I ran out of time! I could not!
It, he, she, they made me! I cannot! I didn't get around to it! Plus
ten thousand other excuses for our inactions and/or actions.
Choices and consequences,
We make choices (for whatever reason/s)
that create consequences (negative or positive),
and those persons in our lives have to choose to accept/contend
or reject/not contend with them.

The Answer

Yes is the answer.

It is the correct response to every conflict, problem, and situation one encounters.

That's right, Even the painful, unwanted, sad, angry, disconcerting, and catastrophic ones.

It is easy to say yes to what we find pleasing/desirable, like, and approve of,

But when you can say yes to everyone and everything, You can be unaffected and, if inclined, make rational decisions

That effectively mitigate and/or eliminate what you find discordant.

When you say yes, you acknowledge and accept every individual, societal, and universal truth/reality,

which allows you to flow instead of suffering the many negative consequences of resistance/denial.

The Book by the Cover
The Love by the Lover

If you possess self-trust,
you can express, give, and permit trust.
If you possess self-security,
you can express, give, and permit security.
If you possess self-faith,
you can express, give, and permit faith.
If you possess self-honesty,
you can express, give, and permit honesty.
If you possess self-love,
you can express, give, and permit love.
If you possess self-acceptance,
You can express, give, and permit acceptance.

If you possess self-reliance,
you can express, give, and permit reliance.

If you possess self-freedom,
You can give, express and permit freedom.

That's Entertainment

Razzle me! Dazzle me! Dance for me! Prance for me!
Woo me! Coo me! Act for me!
Excite me! Swing for me! Punch for me! Run for me!
Impress me! Dress for me! Caress me! Jump for me! Swirl for
me! Entice me! Scintillate me! Perform for me!
Make me giggle, make me wiggle, make me happy, make me sad,
Make me wonder, make me ponder.
My hungry, craving mind is waiting,
my eyes and ears and nose and body funnel your stimulation.
They are impatient, ever ready to be fed, triggered, and turned on.
We hustle and bustle
To theaters, stages, arenas, tents, diamonds, fields, rings, and
pavilions, park, pay the price, and demand expect perfect, excellent
performances (mind does not want to be bored).
We may get hostile, aggressive, and violent if it is not delivered.

Why? Could it be that these are distractions,
Diversions from ourselves, issues, relationships, societal problems?
"Inner-tainment" is free, always accessible, has no static, and
requires no batteries.
One has only to tune in to the love and bliss that pervades the
universe.
Afterward, the entertainments pale in comparison.
Try this airwave, this frequency, tune in, "change" the channel.

A Reminder

Fellow gods and goddesses, please consider, acknowledge, accept,
and embrace the fact
that NO-thing is more important or valuable than you,
Including every award, relationship, class, career, exam, licensure,
certification trophy, material possession, promotion, league,
organization, car, home, social status, and every mandate of
"S.I.C.-ness."
They all take a back seat to and pale against your brilliance, true
worth, heart, and inner essence.

Sun Rises and Sun Sets

Both are fallacies.
You see, like bliss, the sun is ever present. The earth moves, but it is
constant, stationary.
Rises and *sets* are only dramas (or traumas) created by the mass
mind's perception.
Let the sun's eternal radiation remind you of your
Brilliance and bliss, and
Shine, shine, shine.

More! More! More!
The More The Better

The more "perceived" control,
the less real, true societal/personal control.

Transitional Objects

Pacifiers,
Thumbs,
Nipples,
Bottles,
Blankets,
Teddy bears,
Parents,
Partners,
Mates,
Pastors,
Priests,
Rabbis,
Gurus,
Psychologists,
Psychiatrists,
Psychotherapists,
Spouses,
Bests friends,
Lovers,
Healers,
Religions,
Sects,

And
Any other place, person, or thing one runs to for solace
And/or advice.
For they all eventually have to be fired, relinquished, and released,
And let go to chart your own course, weave your own tapestry,
Sing your
own song, dance your own dance, paint your own picture,
Direct your own play, write your own story, play your own game,
Climb your own mountain, soar on your own wings,
and
reach your own highest heights.
Because you and only you know what you must do or not do
To be happy in your heart, satisfied and content with your existence/
life.
And you will also realize that you are whole and complete,
Your self-love, approval, and appreciation are all you really require/need.

The More B

The more self-preoccupation,
the more indifference to other's issues, concerns, problems, and
feelings.

Cosmic Affirmations

I only accept peace, joy, and love from others;
I am balance manifesting.
My higher god/goddess (good) self-guides me on this earth plane;
I am wisdom manifesting.
Beautiful distractions do not sway me from my goals and bliss;
I am peace manifesting,
I am happiness manifesting.
I don't have problems or conflicts, only challenges and
opportunities;
I own my personal power,
I am harmony manifesting.
Others do not define my truths or realities;
I am love manifesting,
I am joy manifesting,
I am achieving my goals.

I am bliss manifesting.

The More C

The more money,
the more worry about where to spend it,
who to trust, paying too many taxes, and toys.

P's

(Think of, or conjure up, your personal and perhaps private positive associations for each word.)

Peach
Peace
Peacock
Profound
Psychic
Pearl
Promise
Positive
Posture
Perform
Pansy
Prevention
Prolific
Pleasant
Pristine
Pure

Purple
Practice
Purse
Perfect
Place
Placid
Prayer
Pretty
Pear
Park
Pj's
Pinky
Pebble
Plenty
Poopsie
Produce
Primrose
Point
Put

Pumpkin

Plant

Purchase

Perchance

Plants

Perhaps

Pilgrimage

Period

Peruse

Poetic

Passion

Permission

Pocket

Polite

Post

Playing

Probable

Present

Progress

Planet

Perch
Presence
People
Paris
Pinch
Personal
Pine Cone
Pleased
Pluto
Poignant
Purpose
Pervade
Practical
Perfume
Package
Pick
Paradise
Pact
Parent

Pen

Phonic

Pinnacle

Prophet

Philosophical

Pontificate

Phenomenal

Philanthropic

P,_____

P,_____

P,_____.

The More D

The more pride,

the more chances for it to get trampled.

Sincerity

Sincerity simplifies your life
and prevents confusion, conflicts, and strife.
It's risky to say what you feel,
but is the honest way to deal.

Co-workers, lovers, family, and friends
will respect you more in the end.

You have the right to be who you are
and will reach all goals faster and easier by far.

So don't be cloudy with your opinions,
feelings, and ideas,
especially when someone wants to hear.
With what's in your heart, head, and soul be
clear,
for smoother sailing every day of the year.

The More E

The more addiction(s),
the more manipulation, effort, and dishonest,
deceitful, illegal tactics
to find, get, and store/keep
it/them.

Attachment vs. Connection

We humans have a habit of attaching to one another and things (tangible and intangible).

This proves to be problematic
because inevitably he/she changes and it gets lost stolen or broken.
Hence, one must deal with painful detachment.
Tissue is broken when a tick is detached from a dog,
when cancerous cells are removed from the body,
when lichen is removed from a tree or stone, much like the
emotional ripping and trauma that occurs when we detach.

Whereas connections are cleaner, easier, and more flexible.
Connections can be changed and altered without damage, friction,
and discomfort.
Consequently, we can have many, move when they become
undesirable, and reconnect with ease.
Hummingbirds connect with numerous flowers,
taking nectar and
spreading pollen. Dancers connect with different partners. Prides,
packs, pods, herds, and schools connect for strength and protection
and may disconnect to mate and raise their offspring.
Electrical appliances can be connected and disconnected in every
room in a house,
in every state and mostly every country on the planet.
In countless ways, connections create greater calmness,
earnest companionship, and real contentment.

The More F

The more holding in/on,

the less letting go/freedom.

Terremotto (Quaking)

When the earth moves or any other disturbing event occurs, their vibrations resound in our minds and souls. This shakes up whatever we have stored there. The contents come crashing down upon us, which makes us confront and face issues we have avoided/blocked/denied or distorted. Often this evokes anxiety, fear, anger, helplessness, persecution, and frustration.

If/when one has a quiet, rational, clear, concentrated, and tranquil mind along with a serene, sated/satisfied, ascended, free, and enlightened soul, there is nothing on the shelves to fall down, be revealed, or traumatize her/him. Therefore, you can remain calm and be unmoved by any catastrophe occurring around you.

The More G

The more ego,

the less self-esteem.

Simple Sexuality
(mutual pleasuring)

Celibate or Bi(sex)ual or Hetero(sex)ual or Homo(sex)ual. This word and these prefixes have been given great social and political power when in fact the only issue is sex. What does it matter? Why should anyone care about or be concerned with what two (or more) consenting (holistically), balanced beings do with their bodies? Moralistic, political, indoctrinated, and religious factions dictate with whom, when, where, how, the frequency, and if mutual pleasuring is right or wrong, good or bad, appropriate or inappropriate, or is a sin. Do we own our bodies? Do you own yours? Maybe it is time to decide.

The More h

The more "Winners"

the more losers.

Equilibrium

All systems seek and struggle for equilibrium.
The human body is one and has many within it
and is usually connected to other ones,
so arc all life forms and their
respective groupings, and planet earth is a system that maintains
and houses millions more.

When a system becomes imbalanced by any form of toxin,
e.g., chemical, intellectual, spiritual, it will first try to cleanse itself.
If one or we continue to replenish the poison, it adapts as much as it can
but becomes weaker and less effective.

Here's hoping that you are putting and permitting healthy,
productive,
growth-enhancing materials in you and your system(s)
along with the society,
the environment, the country,
the planet, and the cosmos, universe.